W9-ARF-445

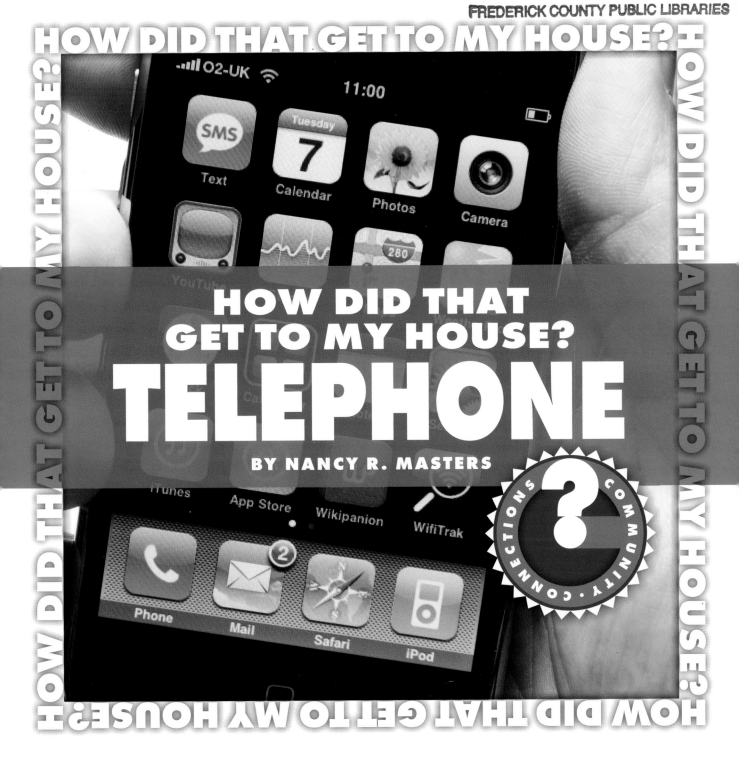

HOW DID THAT GET TO MY HOUSE?
TELEPHONE

BY NANCY R. MASTERS

COMMUNITY · CONNECTIONS

Published in the United States of America by Cherry Lake Publishing
Ann Arbor, Michigan
www.cherrylakepublishing.com

Content Adviser: Mary Raber, Associate Director, Institute for Interdisciplinary Studies, Michigan Technological University
Reading Adviser: Cecilia Minden-Cupp, PhD, Literacy Consultant

Photo Credits: Cover and page 1, ©ICP/Alamy; page 5, ©Felix Mizioznikov, used under license from Shutterstock, Inc.; page 7, ©M.Brodie/Alamy; page 9, ©JUPITERIMAGES/Comstock Images/Alamy; page 11, ©Dee Hunter, used under license from Shutterstock, Inc.; page 13, ©iStockphoto.com/ictor; page 15, ©iStockphoto.com/ReeselImages; page 17, ©c., used under license from Shutterstock, Inc.; page 19, ©Ellen Isaacs/Alamy; page 21, ©lofoto/Dreamstime.com

LIBRARY OF CONGRESS CATALOGING-IN-PUBLICATION DATA

Masters, Nancy Robinson.
  How did that get to my house? Telephone / by Nancy Robinson Masters.
     p. cm—(Community connections)
  Includes bibliographical references and index.
  ISBN-13: 978-1-60279-480-1
  ISBN-10: 1-60279-480-4
  1. Telephone—Juvenile literature. I. Title. II. Title: Telephone. III. Series.
  TK6165.M37 2010
  621.385—dc22   2008054510

Cherry Lake Publishing would like to acknowledge the work of The Partnership for 21st Century Skills. Please visit www.21stcenturyskills.org for more information.

TELEPHONE

CONTENTS

WHAT IS A TELEPHONE?

Rrrring! You hear bells. Blink! You see a flashing light. Buzz! Your hand feels a tingle.

These are signals made by telephones. We use telephones to talk with people. We also use telephones to send text messages and play games. Some telephones even work as computers!

We use telephones to talk with people nearby or far away.

4

5

Telephones have three main parts. They are the microphone, the receiver, and the keypad. You speak into the microphone. You use the receiver, or speaker, to listen. You use the keypad to press in the telephone number of the person you want to call.

What parts of the phone can you see in this picture?

You answer a telephone when you hear it ring. Sometimes phones don't ring. They flash a light or **vibrate** instead. Why do you think someone would want a phone that flashes or vibrates instead of rings?

LANDLINE TELEPHONES

Landline telephones send and receive information. They use electricity. They have cords that plug into **phone jacks**. Phone jacks are found on the walls inside houses. Wires inside the walls connect the phone jacks to telephone power boxes. The power boxes are on the outside walls of houses.

A landline telephone cord is plugged into a phone jack.

More wires connect the power boxes to **transmission cables**. Signals travel along these cables. The cables pass through **switching stations**. There are computers in the switching stations. These computers send the signals where they need to go.

Tall poles of wood or metal hold some telephone lines.

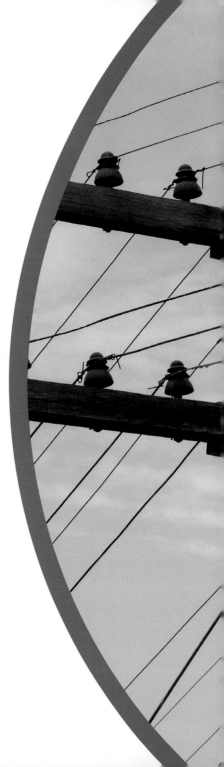

Some transmission cables are **fiber optic** cables. They are made of thin glass or plastic. Fiber optic cables carry signals much faster than wire cables.

Fiber optic transmission cables are buried underground.

LOOK!

Most telephone transmission cables are buried underground. Do you want to know where the cables for your phone are buried? Look for signs near your house that tell where the cables are buried.

13

CELL PHONES

Radio waves are in the air around us all the time. We can't see radio waves. A cell phone is a kind of radio. It does not need to plug into a phone jack. It does not need any wires. It uses battery power to send and receive signals on radio waves.

You can use a cell phone almost anywhere.

15

There is a tiny computer in the cell phone. It sends signals to the nearest **base station**. A base station has a tall steel tower. There are **antennas** on the tower. These send and receive radio wave signals. The signals go from tower to tower. Then they go from cell phone to cell phone.

Antennas on tall towers send and receive cell phone signals.

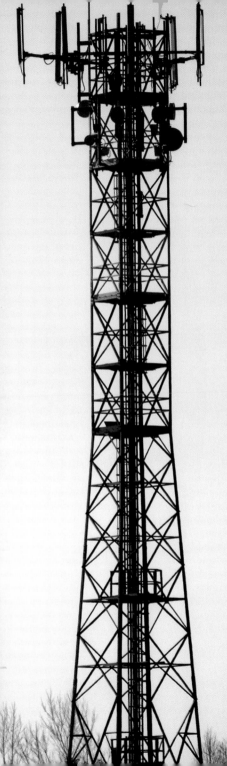

Each cell phone has a special code. The cell phone's antenna collects the signals that match its code. Cell phone computers change these signals back into sounds.

Cell phones don't work if there are no antennas nearby. More towers for antennas are being built to solve this problem.

Cell phones have gotten smaller over the years. Some have antennas that you can see. Other antennas are inside the phone.

Telephones let you talk to people almost anywhere in the world. What kind of phone do you have in your house? Who will you call today?

Phones make it easy to share our lives with others.

Ask an adult to show you the cell tower closest to your house. Talk about how landline telephones and cell phones are different. How are they alike?

GLOSSARY

antennas (an-TEN-uhz) pieces of metal used to send and receive radio wave signals

base station (BAYSS STAY-shuhn) a place with equipment for sending and receiving radio wave signals

fiber optic (FYE-bur OP-tik) a bundle of thin glass or plastic tubes used to carry telephone signals

phone jacks (FOHN JAKS) connectors that link a landline phone to the phone transmission wires

switching stations (SWICH-ing STAY-shuhnz) places that send landline phone signals to the correct phone lines

transmission cables (transs-MISH-uhn KAY-buhlz) bundles of wire or fiber optics that carry landline telephone signals to switching stations

vibrate (VYE-brate) to move back and forth very quickly

FIND OUT MORE

BOOKS

Banting, Erinn. *Inventing the Telephone*. New York: Crabtree Publishing Company, 2006.

McLeese, Don. *Cell Phones*. Vero Beach, FL: Rourke Publishing, 2009.

WEB SITES

ESA Kids—Useful Space: TV and Phones
www.esa.int/esaKIDSen/SEMDSKXJD1E_UsefulSpace_0.html
Learn more about communication satellites

FCC Kids Zone—FAQs
www.fcc.gov/cgb/kidszone/faqs_k3.html
Answers to frequently asked questions about phone communications

INDEX

ABOUT THE AUTHOR

Nancy Robinson Masters has landline telephones and cell phones in her house. She uses both to talk with people all over the world.

24